# HITTING THE SHOT

## THE MOST CLUTCH MOMENTS IN SPORTS

by Eric Braun

CAPSTONE PRESS
a capstone imprint

Published by Capstone Press, an imprint of Capstone
1710 Roe Crest Drive, North Mankato, Minnesota 56003
capstonepub.com

Library of Congress Cataloging-in-Publication Data
Names: Braun, Eric, 1971- author.
Title: Hitting the shot : the most clutch moments in sports / by Eric Braun.
Description: North Mankato, Minnesota : Capstone Press, [2023] | Series: Sports illustrated kids. Heroes and heartbreakers | Includes bibliographical references and index. | Audience: Ages 8-11 | Audience: Grades 4-6 | Summary: "Buzzer-beaters, walk-off homers, and more! In this Sports Illustrated Kids book, discover the all-time greatest clutch moments in sports history. Discover more about Christian Laettner's last-second shot in the 1992 NCAA men's basketball tournament. Read about how Kerri Strug landed a near-perfect vault performance on an injured ankle, helping the U.S. gymnastics team win gold at the 1996 Summer Olympics. Find out how the "Hail Mary" football play first got its name in a 1975 NFL game with just seconds left. With eye-popping photographs and heart-pounding text, this book is sure to attract sports enthusiasts, young and old"— Provided by publisher.
Identifiers: LCCN 2022029293 (print) | LCCN 2022029294 (ebook) | ISBN 9781669011088 (hardcover) | ISBN 9781669011033 (paperback) | ISBN 9781669011040 (pdf) | ISBN 9781669011064 (kindle edition)
Subjects: LCSH: Sports—Juvenile literature. | Sports—Psychological aspects—Juvenile literature.
Classification: LCC GV705.4 .B734 2023 (print) | LCC GV705.4 (ebook) |DDC 796—dc23/eng/20220714
LC record available at https://lccn.loc.gov/2022029293
LC ebook record available at https://lccn.loc.gov/2022029294

Editorial Credits
Editor: Carrie Sheely; Designer: Elyse White; Media Researcher: Donna Metcalf; Production Specialist: Whitney Schaefer

Image and Design Element Credits
Associated Press: 9, Eric Risberg, 25, Harry Cabluck, 5, JOHN GAPS III, 15, Uncredited, 27; Getty Images: adventtr, cover (background), Al Tielemans, 14, Bettmann, 11, Damian Strohmeyer, 29 (top), Hector Mata, 18, Jed Jacobsohn, 7, Joey Mcleister/Star Tribune, 19, Shutterstock: IYIKON, design element (boxing icon), Kanjanee Chaisin, cover (bottom), kuroksta, design element (soccer icon), Martial Red, design element (stopwatch icon), Palsur, design element (icons), Rauf Akhundof, design element (gymnastics icon); Sports Illustrated: Heinz Kluetmeier, 21, 23, Manny Millan, 13, 29 (bottom left), Robert Beck, 17

Source Notes
Page 7, "It was obviously . . . " AZ Snake Pit. "Arizona Diamondbacks All-Time Top 50: #3, Luis Gonzalez," February 17, 2018, https://www.azsnakepit.com/2018/2/17/16939896/arizona-diamondbacks-all-time-top-50-3-luis-gonzalez
Page 22, "Do you believe . . . " U.S. Hockey Hall of Fame. "The 1980 U.S. Olympic Team," https://www.ushockeyhalloffame.com/page/show/831562-the-1980-u-s-olympic-team
Page 27, "It was a Hail Mary . . . " Phil Sheridan, "How Roger Staubach and Drew Pearson Made the 'Hail Mary' Pass Famous," August 6, 2021, https://www.history.com/news/hail-mary-pass-roger-staubach-drew-pearson-1975
Websites accessed March 2022.

# TABLE OF CONTENTS

Words in **bold** are in the glossary.

# PRESSURE AND PERFORMANCE

When the pressure's on, some athletes struggle. But others rise to the occasion. They do something improbable. Something incredible. Something amazing at the perfect time. Those athletes are **clutch**. Those *moments* are clutch.

There are two ingredients to a clutch moment. First, it has to be a moment of great pressure. Maybe something big happens in the final seconds of a game. It might be the deciding play of a world championship. Or perhaps an athlete's career or legacy is at stake. Whatever causes the pressure, it needs to be sky-high.

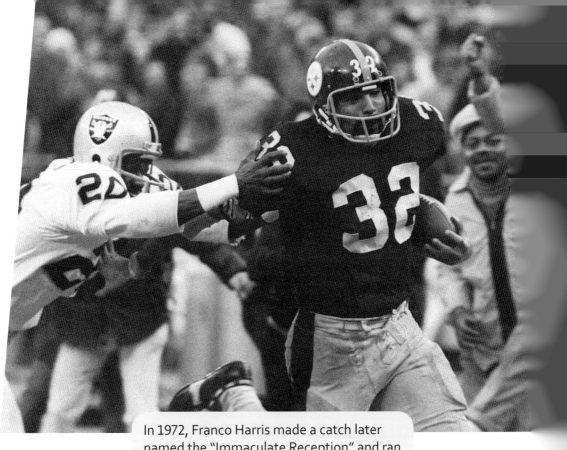

In 1972, Franco Harris made a catch later named the "Immaculate Reception" and ran for a touchdown. It gave Pittsburgh the lead with seconds left in an NFL playoff game.

Ingredient number two is that an athlete needs to do something great. Not just above average. Not just pretty good. It needs to be awesome.

Clutch moments are what fans always hope to see. Let's look at some of the biggest clutch moments in history.

# CHAPTER 1
# RISING TO THE OCCASION

You want to be the best? You have to *beat* the best. These stories highlight athletes who had the odds stacked against them. And then they came up clutch.

## LUIS GONZALEZ WALKS IT OFF

Picture this: It's Game 7 of the 2001 World Series. It's the bottom of the 9th inning, and the game is tied 2–2. The bases are loaded. And standing on the mound is baseball's greatest relief pitcher—the New York Yankees' Mariano Rivera.

The Arizona Diamondbacks had to score a run to keep the game from going into extra innings. The Yankees were an absolute machine. They'd won four of the last five World Series. Rivera was already a **legend**.

As the Diamondbacks' Luis Gonzalez stepped into the box, the hometown crowd cheered him on. Then, on an 0–1 pitch, he hit a single up the middle to bring in the winning run. "It was obviously a childhood dream come true," Gonzalez later said.

Gonzalez swings at a pitch during Game 7 of the 2001 World Series.

## A HEALING WORLD SERIES

The 2001 World Series took place just a few weeks after terrorists attacked the United States on September 11. After the attacks, no baseball was played for almost two weeks. When the games started again, it helped heal a hurting nation. The Diamondbacks had their World Series rings engraved with "9-11-01 Never Forget."

## CASSIUS CLAY ARRIVES

In 1960, a new pro boxer arrived on the scene. He was a loudmouth. A braggart. A joker. A showoff. Who was he?

His name was Cassius Clay. In the world of boxing, he was a nobody. Yet he still called himself "The Greatest."

Clay's excellent boxing record earned him the right to challenge Sonny Liston, the heavyweight champion of the world. Clay proclaimed that he would defeat Liston by knocking him out in eight rounds.

In 1962, Liston had defeated the previous heavyweight champ by knocking him out in the first round. In their rematch the next year, he did it again. Experts said that nobody had ever hit harder than Sonny Liston.

Clay (left) with his brother Rahman in May 1964

But that didn't matter to Clay. He said that if Liston won, he would kiss Liston's feet and leave the country. How's that for pressure?

When the fight started on February 25, 1964, Liston couldn't land a solid punch. Clay jabbed and moved. He wore Liston out. Experts and fans were surprised. However, Clay wasn't able to knock out Liston in the eighth round. Why? Because Liston gave up before the seventh round even began!

Cassius Clay was no longer a nobody.

**FUN FACT**

Soon after the February 1964 fight, Clay changed his name to Muhammad Ali.

Clay shouts out after defeating Liston and winning the heavyweight boxing title in February 1964.

## KERRI STRUG STICKS THE LANDING

The U.S. Women's Gymnastics team was in a good position. At the 1996 Summer Olympics, they had a chance to upset Russia and win gold. Going back to 1952, the Russian team had won nine out of 11 gold medals in the women's all-around team event.

But with only the **vault** routine left, Team USA had the chance to win. It all came down to the last vaulter, Kerri Strug. She needed a score of 9.493. If she met that, the U.S. would win gold. If she fell short, it would go to Russia.

Pressure? Yeah, a little bit.

### FUN FACT

The Soviet Union was a country until December 1991. Since then, the country has been called Russia.

Strug performs on the balance beam at the 1996 Summer Olympics.

On Strug's first attempt, her leg buckled on the landing and she heard a snap. She didn't know it yet, but she had torn **ligaments** in her ankle. All she knew was that it hurt—bad. And the gold medal was hanging in the balance.

Strug limped back for her second attempt. The terrible pain was written on her face. But somehow, she found the strength to run and launch herself off the springboard. She performed a nearly perfect vault and stuck the landing—on one good foot.

Strug was in a lot of pain after injuring her ankle.

The crowd went wild as Strug fell to the floor in pain. Then the score came in: 9.712. More than enough to win the gold. It was an incredible clutch moment in Olympic history.

The 1996 U.S. Olympic gymnastics team members wave to the crowd after receiving their gold medals.

# CHAPTER 2
# MORE THAN SPORTS

Sports give us great stories. There are killer comebacks, thrilling victories, and dramatic losses. But some sports stories are more important than the action on the field. Sometimes sports can change the world.

## A KICK FOR WOMEN'S SPORTS

The final game of the 1999 Women's World Cup was held in the Rose Bowl in Pasadena, California. The sold-out stadium was rocking as the U.S. team faced China for the title.

The game was a tense, defensive battle. The two teams were tied 0–0 at the end of regulation time. The winner would be decided by penalty kicks. The score was tied 4–4 as Brandi Chastain took the final shot for the United States. The championship rested on her as the crowd of more than 90,000 looked on. Talk about pressure.

After Chastain took her shot, the fans in the crowded stadium looked on in anticipation.

When Chastain took her kick, the ball sailed past the goalie and into the net. Victory! Chastain tore off her jersey and swung it over her head to celebrate. Then she dropped to her knees, her face showing pure joy. She—and the U.S. team—had not just won the Women's World Cup. They brought women's sports into the world spotlight.

Chastain reacts after kicking the game-winning goal in the 1999 Women's World Cup.

People demonstrate at a basketball game in support of Title IX.

## TITLE IX

In 1972, a law called Title IX was passed. It said that no public school could exclude someone from playing sports based on their sex. It meant that women's sports should be treated the same as men's sports. However, men's sports continued to get more attention than women's sports. Many consider the 1999 World Cup to be the first time that people truly saw how popular women's sports could be.

## THE MIRACLE ON ICE

In the 1980 Winter Olympics, nobody expected the U.S. hockey team to go far. The Soviet Union's team was heavily favored to win the gold medal. It was the best hockey team in the world. The Soviets had won gold in the past four Winter Olympics.

But the U.S. team wasn't going down without a fight. When the two teams met in the medal round, the Soviets went up 2–1 as time ticked away in the first period. But then Dave Christian launched a desperation shot from the far end of the ice. The puck bounced off the Soviet goalie's pads and toward the stick of Mark Johnson.

The Soviets score during the 1980 Winter Olympics.

Johnson snagged the puck, made one quick fake, and popped it into the net as time expired. It was only the end of the first period, but Johnson's shot would prove to be the clutch moment of the contest. It showed that the Americans meant business.

Team USA led 4–3 as the final seconds of the game ticked off the clock. That's when announcer Al Michaels gave the historic call: "Do you believe in miracles? Yes!" Two days later, the United States defeated Finland to win the gold.

## SCORE ONE FOR DEMOCRACY

The victory over the Soviet Union was more important for the United States than just winning an Olympic hockey game. The two nations were fierce political rivals, and the most powerful in the world. To many Americans, victory on the ice felt like a victory for **democracy** over the Soviet Union's **communist** government.

The U.S. men's Olympic hockey team celebrates after winning the semifinal game in 1980.

# CHAPTER 3
# SO CLUTCH THEY GOT A NAME

Some plays become instant classics. Legends in their own time—and for all time. These are the plays that are so clutch they got a nickname. Just hearing that name can give fans goosebumps.

## THE "FLIP PLAY"

It was Game 3 of the 2001 American League Division Series. The Yankees were down two games to none against the Oakland Athletics. New York was clinging to a 1–0 lead in the bottom of the 7th inning. Then Oakland left fielder Terrence Long blasted a line drive to the right field corner. Jeremy Giambi, who had been on first base, rounded second, and then third.

Yankees right fielder Shane Spencer threw wildly toward the infield. Meanwhile, Derek Jeter ran toward the first baseline.

As Giambi lumbered toward home, Spencer's throw went over the head of the cutoff man. It bounced once and landed in Jeter's glove, who was in the perfect spot. Still running, he flipped the ball backhand to catcher Jorge Posada. Posada swiped the tag on Giambi as he tried to score. Out!

The Yankees held on to win that game and then the series. They made it all the way to Game 7 of the World Series before falling to the Diamondbacks.

Posada makes the tag just before Giambi gets to home plate during Game 3 of the 2001 American League Division Series.

## THE "HAIL MARY"

The term for a long, desperate football pass is commonly known as a "Hail Mary" today. But the name first became popular during a game on December 28, 1975.

The Minnesota Vikings were up 14–10 against the Dallas Cowboys in a playoff game. The Cowboys had the ball with just 32 seconds on the clock. They had one last chance and half a field to go.

Dallas receiver Drew Pearson sprinted downfield as quarterback Roger Staubach launched the ball as far as he could. Pearson adjusted to the pass and knocked down Minnesota defender Nate Wright. Pearson caught the ball on the 5-yard line and ran to the end zone for the winning score. The Vikings protested the play. They said that Pearson committed pass interference. But the touchdown stood.

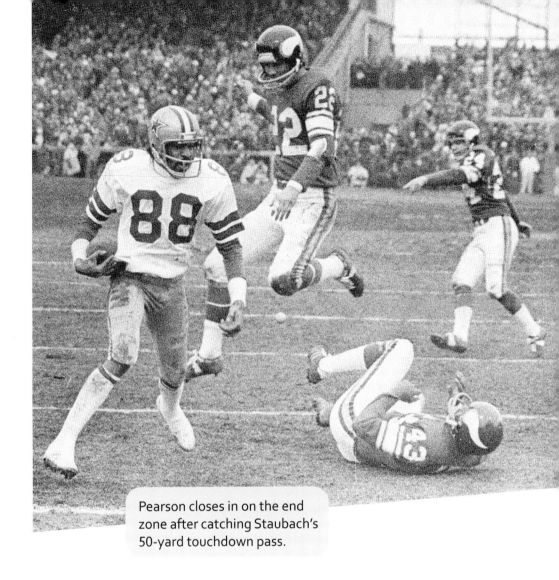

Pearson closes in on the end zone after catching Staubach's 50-yard touchdown pass.

"It was a Hail Mary pass," Staubach told reporters afterward, referring to a Hail Mary prayer. "I just threw it up there as far as I could."

## "THE SHOT"

The year was 1992. The matchup was between Duke and Kentucky. The two teams were NCAA Division I college basketball powerhouses. The hard-fought tournament game went to overtime.

Deep into overtime, Kentucky held a one-point lead. Duke had just 2.1 seconds to take the ball down the court and score a basket. It seemed impossible. Grant Hill lobbed a football-like pass downcourt to Christian Laettner, who leapt above the crowd to grab it. With his back to the basket, Laettner dribbled to his right. Then he turned back to his left, spun around, and took his shot—nothing but net.

Duke won the game as time expired, and they went on to win the tournament. But the team couldn't have done it without "the Shot."

Laettner makes his game-winning shot with just seconds left during the 1992 NCAA tournament.

Duke players celebrate their 1992 championship win with their coach, Mike Krzyzewski.

# GLOSSARY

**clutch** (KLUCH)
when someone does
something great in
a moment of big
pressure

**communist**
(KAHM-yuh-nist)
relating to a country
or person practicing
communism;
communism is a political
system in which there is
no private property, and
everything is owned by
the government

**democracy**
(di-MAH-kruh-see)
a form of government in
which the citizens can
choose their leaders

**legend** (LEJ-uhnd)
someone who is among
the best in what they do

**ligament**
(LIG-uh-muhnt)
a band of tissue that
connects bones to bones

**vault** (VAWLT)
a gymnastics move in
which the gymnast
pushes off a padded
structure called a vault
with their hands and
performs various twists
and flips before landing

# READ MORE

Buckley Jr., James. *Muhammad Ali: The Greatest of All Time!* San Diego: Portable Press, 2020.

Doeden, Matt. *Coming Up Clutch: The Greatest Upsets, Comebacks, and Finishes in Sports History.* Minneapolis: Millbrook Press, 2019.

Terrell, Brandon. *Soccer Showdown: U.S. Women's Stunning 1999 World Cup Win.* North Mankato, MN: Capstone, 2019.

# INTERNET SITES

*Ducksters: Sports Biographies*
ducksters.com/sports.php

*National Baseball Hall of Fame*
baseballhall.org

*Pro Football Hall of Fame*
profootballhof.com

# INDEX

# ABOUT THE AUTHOR

**Eric Braun** is the author of dozens of books for young readers. His favorite things to write about include history, fairy tales, and especially sports. One of his books was read by an astronaut on the International Space Station. Besides stories, he loves bike riding, camping, adventures, and wearing hats. Learn more at heyericbraun.com.